ONE MORE WORLD LIKE THIS WORLD

Also by Carlie Hoffman

This Alaska
When There Was Light

Translations from the German
White Shadows: Anneliese Hager and the Camera-less Photograph

As Editor
Todesfuge/Deathfugue: Pierre Joris & Paul Celan
Small Orange Conversations with Poets, issues 1 & 2

ONE MORE WORLD LIKE THIS WORLD

Carlie Hoffman

Four Way Books
Tribeca

Copyright 2025 Carlie Hoffman

No part of this book may be used or reproduced in any manner without written permission except in the case of brief quotations embodied in critical articles and reviews.

Library of Congress Cataloging-in-Publication Data

Names: Hoffman, Carlie, author.
Title: One more world like this world : poems / Carlie Hoffman.
Description: New York : Four Way Books, 2025.
Identifiers: LCCN 2024037070 (print) | LCCN 2024037071 (ebook) |
ISBN 9781961897281 (trade paperback) | ISBN 9781961897298 (ebook)
Subjects: LCGFT: Poetry.
Classification: LCC PS3608.O47753 O54 2025 (print) | LCC PS3608.O47753 (ebook) | DDC 811/.6--dc23/eng/20240816
LC record available at https://lccn.loc.gov/2024037070
LC ebook record available at https://lccn.loc.gov/2024037071

This book is manufactured in the United States of America and printed on acid-free paper.

Four Way Books is a not-for-profit literary press. We are grateful for the assistance we receive from individual donors, public arts agencies, and private foundations including the New York State Council on the Arts, a state agency.

We are a proud member of the Community of Literary Magazines and Presses.

Contents

After Translating the Women of the 20th Century   3

I.

THE GARDEN

A Condo for Sale Overlooking the Cemetery in Kearny, NJ   7
Borges Sells Me the Apple, Sells Me the World   10
Memory of France   11
November Morning on Graham Avenue   12
The Wolves Ran on Through the Evergreen Forests   13
I'll Give This Letter to a Worm   14
The Townspeople Contemplate Eurydice   15
Ode to the Sudden Forgetting of Your Grief   17
Author's Myth   20

II.

THE REPLICA

Author's Myth   25
Reading Virginia Woolf in a Women in Literature Class at Bergen
    Community College   26
Moses in Brooklyn   31
Inventory   32
Driving Through Maspeth, NY, After Teaching an Introduction to Creative
    Writing Class   34
Teaching the Persona Poem at Ramapo College of New Jersey   36
Myth of Icarus as Girl, Leaving   37
The Year Made Out of a Cut in Your Civilization   39
The Twenty-First Century   40
The Twenty-First Century   41
Refurbished Eden   42
Panorama After Foreclosure   45

III.

THEN ROSES

Point of View Where Orpheus Makes a Pit Stop at a Fortune Teller in
   St. Germain 49
Mary Magdalene, Mary Oliver, & Me 50
Rose Ausländer, Jane Roe, & Me 52
Twentieth-Century Novel 55
At the CarMax in Maryland to Sell Your Used Civic That Doesn't Have
   Air Conditioning but was Your Grandmother's and the Only Place
   You've Ever Owned 56
Eden in Foreclosure 57
New World: Eurydice 59
A Legend and Its Context 60
Borges Sells Me the Apple, Sells Me the World 62

Notes

"And the sea?"

"It's too far."

"And home?"

"Also."

—*Elena Ferrante (translated by Ann Goldstein)*

After Translating the Women of the 20th Century

A prayer

This winter I want a house
where women glide from god's photographs:
their prewar radios and Eastern fields renounced

of stars and the memory of cows,
their lockets filled with a history of grass.
This winter I want a house

and in it, the clock ticks near the window, sound
leaking like bad oil and watch how the curtain sops
the smell of the past. This winter I want a house

with a garden and one rose
like a lipsticked girl chewing a match.
This winter I want a house.

She brings in flowers waiting without
rain, dazzling at the root in a bath—
a metaphor of this winter house.

A green stem behind her ear in the past
where the women glide from god's photographs.
This winter I want a house.
She is playing music when god is renounced.

I.
THE GARDEN

A Condo for Sale Overlooking the Cemetery in Kearny, NJ

You must imagine Eurydice
      happy, that hell, too,
is an industrious world: round

dining table alive
      with breadcrumbs, rabbits
handed off one morning

on someone's
      front porch, an Eastern sun
bleating down across

blunted ax lines
      blurred like letters
on an optometrist's screen. You need

to consider what she gave
      to herself, if you move
through this world again, caught

between the rainbowed bridge traffic
      of delivery trucks—staggered fish
headed north for winter.

Here you leave
        the dishes in the sink
of an apartment where

the rent's gone
        too high and, still wanting
to stay a while, you believe

in this glimmer of land
        among the car repair shops,
the sewage plant, overlooking

the parking lot and graveyard's
        fertile grass. This is where,
finally, so much life

on your hands,
        you will sleep: Eurydice knew
where she was going—

her white gown
        blown downward, her music
bleeding from the inside, out.

A blushed snow fox
        descending through the farm's
technology. She didn't

leave the light
        but swallowed it,
demanding a better song.

Borges Sells Me the Apple, Sells Me the World

In the blizzard
of my life

nothing moved me, my voice
an empty basin, stone

taking on the mouth's shape.
If I heard music

it was a sound from below, vibration
thickening from under the earth.

I drew the apples one by one
knowing they would be a disappointment.

It is not expression I long for,
but the apple

just before. Imagine
believing what you know so forcefully

you will live this blizzard
all your life for this apple.

Memory of France

After Paul Celan

I miss Paris when it rains, I miss the myth
of flower girls selling futures, bleak horse
with its music breaking down:
You lose the lottery. I leave for the sea.
Grass grows between the cobblestones
where we once stood, unrelating.
The room is raining, each petal
a beautiful hoof. You tune
the chrysanthemum. I wear water
as my blue apron, shaking
your heart from my hair.

November Morning on Graham Avenue

The neighbor is playing Chopin again.
I keep the curtain closed. My favorite part

is already knowing the cold outside. Yesterday,
walking back from the store, sadness

flew toward me from a bag of leaves,
invisible sound so beautiful I could have

dropped my apples in the street and cried.
I haven't had enough money or love of money

for a very long time. I put the coffee on
and open the encyclopedia to a confident age—

bombarded city with its chair in the sun,
piano glowing with people approaching

astonishment in a room from long ago—
where the dead go, they leave music behind.

The Wolves Ran on Through the Evergreen Forests

Little monster on my lap, your song is broken, unbearable,
and the roofs of this town grow invisible vines

toward a backward story. I feel failed here. The wolves
are lonely, unable to reach the God who sneers

from the mountain's edge. Together,
we peer at the frozen trees, unreflective.

I could snap
the root with my thumb, but instead,

I travel with you into
the greening history and when the downpour arrives

I am glad for the rain always happening
in the past. I am certain of the rose I carry

underneath language where music stops:
I am giving you a better brain.

I'll Give This Letter to a Worm

After Sarah Ruhl

Letter in the frothing field of cornflower & tiger's milk.

Letter among forsythia & speckled trout.

Letter with misplaced brain, its telephone's delphic ringing.

Letter swimming haphazardly toward the albacore & blue fish & basking shark.

Letter stringing hawk moth to whalebone singing the Lord.

Letter's weathervane of thunder snake & blacksnake & cottonmouth &
    sidewinder & cobra.

Letter hungry for ant lion, preying locust in sun.

Letter foxlike & bassarisk, resurrecting.

At the scene of disaster: fireworm, earthworm, shipworm.

No day is new in the name of the Lord who knows language

is a person-sized regret—no day is safe from news of me.

The Townspeople Contemplate Eurydice

When September ends
the woman is

alone again,
brushing

her teeth
beneath the bleached

light in her boring
underwear, an orchid

opening underground
like that Russian poet

who wished
to be buried

alive
beneath an oak tree. Unusual

desire, even for a Romantic,
but the woman's moon

descends the smokestacks
where she finally swims

the sea again. The selfish,
mint-tinged sea.

O, the woman is a glorious fish.

Her mind goes on
uncontrollably.

Her toothbrush
the scythe—

her mind
is the blood of the tree.

Ode to the Sudden Forgetting of Your Grief

I arrive as night falls   as a goldfinch plummets

      to your feet like an old newspaper
      like someone in a pool hall dropping

the yellow ball

              as heavy as carrying
              the pot of soup across a long

hallway when it is dark

      and you are grateful for the moon
      whose face you recognize,

even here, even now,   as the cow lies frozen in the field

and the past swarms with its style and fire

        the way people swarm

              when they are worried or
              afraid

of what comes next
though it's only either flood or fire,

the earth scorched in a rush   as mothers in winter
carry groceries to the car,   the children witnessing

so much work in an instant they are   almost invisible,

almost the oxen
lumbering down the hill

in a violet stream   as in a song I knew but have newly

forgotten as in my tongue
weakens its knowing

like a worn-out penny as in lightning
dims beautiful November,

as in the squirrels fidget their   sharp-muscled geometries as I arrive in the falling forest as I   think to scavenge the dictionary

for this word but it is not language
clearing the landscape

                         of what I've known.

Author's Myth

Despite loving the strawberries for how they are wild-
ly beautiful. Because one of all
the animals in you holds her magnifying glass above the ant hill, wielding
    the sun. Because human authority

is insufficient. Despite how good it feels looking fishlike at the walls
of the Synagogue. Because instead of strawberries the Rabbi's ocean mouth.

There is the God in you peeling your shell like a toenail.
There is the fishhooked God in you like a question mark.

Because Moses knew the sea upon arrival. Before Carmel and the suicides.
The sand keeps you
warm. After Moses the logger knowing

a way out of the nowhere
of the valley. Despite the mountain is nothing and the only
way through. Not every animal can survive this

but there is a tree you cannot name. Its voice glows out of nature, you must
    attempt,
(because it can't
be read), where

an ocean begins at the beginning and not every animal can.

II.

THE REPLICA

Author's Myth

Not every animal can begin at the beginning where an ocean can't
be read. Out of nature

a voice glows like a tree survived out of all

the unnamed animals. When Moses knew his way through
the valley, the sand

was warm. Before Carmel and the suicides. After
the sea. God was a fisherman above the world. The Rabbi opened his throat

and the ocean swelled. God gave you feet and you emerged in the Synagogue
despite comprehending the fishlike walls. You are sufficient in the sun's
                                        authority, human of all
the animals.

The strawberries are beautifully wild and you love—

Reading Virginia Woolf in a Women in Literature Class at Bergen Community College

I know it's October because I wear
shoes without socks. The air is good
to me & I sweat less through my shirts.
Entire days of trees on campus, of stray geese
crowding the grass near the traffic
circle like groupies, as if
the honking cars were a rock band.
It's October & Keith, my high school
crush, waves from the back
of the classroom. I have no idea why
he's here, the radiator hissing
at his back, except the cliché of boys
who always return from where they've
left, like Odysseus but less
plagued by spring & the sea, the mis-
understanding of his nature but I never
asked him & now something inside
me shifts off balance even though
my stomach's been twisted
for hours but I'm so hopped up
on coffee & Midol that I have no point
of view & the afternoon becomes a mood
tilting toward Keith like shifting weight
from one foot to the other, he is

obnoxiously here & he fucked
my older sister, I am just now
remembering, though this was a few
years ago & long after the day I'd
tagged along to go apple picking,
dirt from the groves still
in my nails late at night
when my sister asked if I'd ever
kissed anyone. I was just beginning
freshman year, working to get my time
down for swim team where I'd spent summer
ditching birthdays & the ice cream
truck's persuasive tune to practice
the butterfly & freestyle & learning to dive
less crooked, which was going as well
as expected until Andrew
sat next to me on the bus
ride home from the pool during tryouts,
his chlorine-dried hand on my shoulder
a little too long without asking when he asked
my name & *he has a crush on you*
said my friend Becca while faking
a gagging sound in her throat. I said yes
even though I hadn't kissed anyone & maybe

this was my first true poem, lying
to my sister in support of love, stealing imagery
from the books I'd read in the library
to avoid the cafeteria: a girl at camp
gets fingered in the lake. A girl goes
missing & is happy being
gone, a little grateful, even. Even before
Shakespeare & Lavinia, Ovid & Philomela,
I believed dead girls
lived eternally as trees & on bad-
weather nights their leaves flew into
the gutters, choking the rain pipes:
fishing-boats against the moon,
wrote Woolf on grief;
giant artichokes towered among roses.
The world can be the saddest fish tank.
In the orchard my sister throws an apple
at me then flirts with Keith.
In class his arm means
nothing as I study
admiration, glancing at the girl
three desks ahead who I had seen
at parties, the kind where all the boys
wear V-necks with tight jeans & play music

in bands, smoke weed in the kitchen, controlling
the music, yelling lyrics into a kind
of oblivion, spilling beer on whoever
they've grabbed to dance while I watch
her from my spot against the fridge
as she lights a cigarette & is effort-
lessly cool in her black tuxedo vest, taking
a break from University but keeping up
on credits. She gets invited
to the Stone Pony in Asbury Park
on weeknights to listen
to the boys play their out-of-tune
guitars & she already
read *The Bell Jar*, she tells our professor
who adjusts the volume
for the projector & I am writing
in my notebook: *read The Bell Jar.*
We have just finished
a unit on poetry & are moving on
to prose. The professor shuts the lights
& a woman stands dead-
center on a spot-lit stage without
an audience because *it would have been*
impossible, she says, *for a woman to have*

written the plays of Shakespeare
in the age Shakespeare
had written. I write
this down in my notebook
because Judith could not & the girl
from the party who has already read
The Bell Jar is staring
out the window while Keith
rests his head in the warmth
of his palm & Andrew rides the bus
to the swim meet where I didn't
make the cut & Becca
has just found out I had sex
before her & she's calling
me a slut & my sister sinks
her teeth into the apple
as the geese applaud
from the lawn & the professor does not
teach us that seven days before
Woolf marries she finishes
this novel & in October
reads it over to
decide whether it is
to go straight into Hell.

Moses in Brooklyn

Bleating, scattered suns of geese
overhead, a flame alphabet:

what is unwritten, hardened
into language, lays bare
a sky. Then the omen

in C-Town on Graham Avenue, lambs
to the left, animal among

the animals. Half-broken figure
bent under the smoke-

feathered sky, day
and night—I

am composing you.

Inventory

At sixteen I worked at a Build-a-Bear in the mall,
stuffing the soft skins

of teddy bears. During my shifts
I sat by a big machine as children lined up

like cars in a drive thru, or hungry mouths
at the counter of my grandparents'

luncheonette in Liberty, New York,
in between wars.

The children looked like children. I wore
a denim button-down and khaki pants. Before stitching

each animal shut, I'd pluck a tiny, satin heart
from a plastic bucket like

a pomegranate seed.
One child made a wish,

then another. It was not for me to ask
what the wish was, only to gesture

to where within the cavern the heart would go.
After closing, just as spring

shadowed the parking lot with the first signs,
I'd bring a pencil and notepad to the back of the store

and take inventory: shelves of toy animal skins stacked
on metal scaffolding—young men sleeping soundly

in the barracks—the stockroom
a cathedral in repair.

Beneath muffled light, I count the hairs
sticking to bottles, the second

used condom, seeds in a pomegranate.
Within his glassy dome, snow is falling

as Hades takes Persephone
deeper inside the replica of girlhood.

Driving Through Maspeth, NY, After Teaching an Introduction to Creative Writing Class

Sun squints off the side
of a delivery truck

like whiskey poured
over a glass of ice

in the Sexton poem where she
is not dead but death's

opposite, being
born and born. Repetition

is the music of memory
but it is also the petition of the dead,

always a place
where the steam from the factories

is the steam from the factory
of girlhood whose gift

you do not yet
know. The doll

in the poem is desire
and terror. You know this

from life, from the forest
in which the terrible

thing that happened scratches
the film of memory

into unbearable
static. You were not born

kneeling. The doll is no longer
before the thing

that happens
which can never be taken back.

Teaching the Persona Poem at Ramapo College of New Jersey

In another poem with a doll, this one by Ai, the speaker's
little sister drags her doll through the mud in the opening
line. The speaker of the poem is a fourteen-year-old
boy, who, just now in the poem, if you want to be
reductive about it, murders his family,
and you can say, as my students are saying, the boy
is a sociopath, which, in life or a newspaper, the boy
could be described as, if this were a headline, but in the poem
the gender roles glare like four sharp corners
of the room, or nuclear family. The sister's muddied doll is a point
of view the speaker takes with him as he packs up and exits
the scene. In class, I ask my students to describe to each other
the feeling of rage before it rises from the body,
if desire rots like an apple without song. Buber believed
the truest *I* does not exist without a *you*, dialogue the place
where desire and expression converge and the animal gallops
extravagantly toward the flame of her knowing. I don't know
if here I am the woman returned to the scene of disaster, transfigured,
the apple inside me rising from the edges of my body as speech.
Outside the classroom window, snow falls, unencumbered
by a wind from nowhere the night Eurydice chooses to stay.

Myth of Icarus as Girl, Leaving

That winter I left the religion with three other girls, my brother wailing
    and wielding the dinner knives, infecting the music

with angry notes. The rabbit outside was incurable, hanging
    in the invisible orchard by an invisible black cord. You could reach

your hand and touch a voice that dire, severed from Earth. Not music,
    but the red fish swimming in the glass tank at night. I float

in the Dead Sea and become pastoral. On Ben Yehuda Street
    the siren blares. It was only a suitcase abandoned in the road.

The other girls and I take cover in a hookah shop. In the morning in Eilat,
    we stretch our arms over the barbed wiring and into the
                    blooming hot air

above Jordan until I am dehydrated, roaming the hotel lobby
    in search of water—*shoteh mayim* said the bus driver who brought us

from Tel Aviv airport to Jerusalem where we prayed for hours
    (our bones grew new bones with little leaves). The other girls
                    and I are making

this a song: drink water, *shoteh mayim*, until the ocean becomes our blood,
we sing
hiking Masada, dried rocks cracking as they make their downward
flight behind us.

This could kill me; will it kill me: nothing like the prophets we learn about
in Sunday school, the thick burning smell seared into our clothes,

the sun's yellow heat tongue-tips our hair. Beyond the acres of pepper fields,
the highways drag gasoline over our skin.

I plant a tree with the certainty my brother will reemerge from beneath the
sea—
How many metaphors less damaging for escaping? How many times

did his call puncture my solitude—the air spinning all around his body,
the holiday meal ruined, the rabbit in the orchard, the fish watching

from the other side of their mirrored life; it seems
the fish keep swimming across the other side of our flooding world.

The Year Made Out of a Cut in Your Civilization

Out of the lamb's eye where the dead
shop for perfumes and bronze-colored cake. Out of
the buttered cobs, embarrassing and sweet corn
in your teeth. Out of a fog
engorged above Baltic waves. The loan-sharked waves. Out of how
happy we all could be. Out of the gun in the girl's dress pocket.
Out of seamstress and the ghost. Out of the unkind,
blond-haired spring where your name goes missing in the wind.
Out of crispy fish skin regressing to oil. Out of your Polish side
draping its scales over your Russian side. Out of the branch's
private misery. Out of your gums, the last leaf
and Yiddish tooth. Out of the refurbished, de-fished sea.

The Twenty-First Century

I watch the lonely wolves
button up

their twentieth-century skins.
They wear history's

violent beauty
like a mother.

The Twenty-First Century

A girl's mouth parts
in the middle of winter

as she turns her back on Bach,
then Heidegger, then returns

to Akhmatova
asking for the indefinite

which is the truth.

Refurbished Eden

Horses neighing in the desert that never

ends. Strawberries from a boreal forest. Bonfire

in the garden where a pot boils for jam. Someone adds

the leaves to a century spinning a silence void of anger.

How a tongue can be a foreign creature thrashing

on its back like a toppled goat or sheep or foal. My father's

mother hides their Russian in cabinets

among the worn-out spoons and sugar bowls. The language

cobwebbed, dehydrated stems peeking out from a sieve—

autumn crocus, peony, siberian lily. His mother

has firm views on everything: here is the right time

to pick a plum. Dark is where the children go

to sleep. Basketball is American, which is good. In Liberty, New York,

       my father hurls his basketball at the garage door then ties

       on his apron and enters his parents' deli

       to sweep away the raisined bodies

of dead flies. His mother has firm views

       on everything: here is an honest man and a man

       who is not. Here is how you grow a garden. My father

counts loose dimes and quarters for customers, pressing his hand

against their palms, and the leaves sprout. He is telling

       my sister and I the story again like potential memory.

He points his broom to the war, the camp, the soldiers who

will order one of us to shoot the other. He holds his staff

like Moses in the garden—*golden root, azalea, siberian lily.*

Go ask Cain, he says. Abel's already written down.

Panorama After Foreclosure

After Federico García Lorca and Yehuda Amichai

I used to think it could be solved this way:
like birds huddled above the U-Haul
along the branch rusting through
its green roof. Skycreatures. Balloon
on the house. My mother shrieks
in the garden. The snake
nude against the light. Here: I give you
my feathers—and here are all
my clouds, the volcano's intimacy—
but the birds aren't ready
to be oxen again, the mountain matted
with Sisyphus' sweat. Always the disdainful
shelves of fruit, which is history. The engine
shivers. The dead stay dead.

III.

THEN ROSES

Point of View Where Orpheus Makes a Pit Stop at a Fortune Teller in St. Germain

I have studied the arithmetic of goodbyes,
calculated the oxen chewing the last line of grass

as the woman and the music merge, indistinguishable.
Of all the forms of divination, I am prone

to numerology, the root of the matter, an ugly
chorus following you as you place your question

in the stone of the city's gate. It will always
hurt, even when the halcyon comes carrying

the sea in her wings. The sundial's been carved
in the dirt. Don't you see

the woman controls your weather now,
each cloud babbling her image,

a faint music, the exit
already closing from below.

Mary Magdalene, Mary Oliver, & Me

After the man at the kosher restaurant called me a whore
in the middle of the day during Sunday service, matzo ball
                                                    soup, & chicken bones

After I held the woman's baby in my Magdalened lap
among the sliced pita & garbage can stinking of chicken bones

After I quit & threw the apron in the trash with the chicken bones

After winter in New Jersey where the main street whispered ice brittle as
                                                    chicken bone

After Bergen Community College & the parking lot, staring at the geese
        overhead like chicken their singing & thinking *to-the-bone singing is*
                                                    their singing

After car breaks down or car crashed into or car broken down after
                                        window cracked & cracking
        the sound of jawing down on chicken bones

After Bank of America crying my paycheck emptied, the overdraft fees,
                                                    my face

        pale as chicken, as bone

After getting work at Applebee's Bar & Grill & doubles & late for class &

                                       skipping class &

    sleeping on grass near the parking lot instead of class &

                             sweeping chicken bones

(Waitressing is chicken bones   between booth cracks, chicken

      bones corner of expo, agonizing

           fish, 3am, 4am, sleep one more hour

                  & forfeit a shower,

section 8 worst section,   L selling oxies near the girl's

bathroom, managers' chicken-bone hands

            on you, you

                now chicken on the bone)

After Gary (the regular) brings me Mary Oliver (*true as Mary Magdalene*

                  creature of desire)

After *when I sit like this, quiet, all the dreams of my blood.* After how *it wasn't*
    about the bird it was something about the way the stone stays mute and put.

Rose Ausländer, Jane Roe, & Me

Much remains to be said, though our garden lies

                                 buried in the cemetery.

I bring stones from the gate

                      of the cities made invisible

and count backward:

                        there is my friend C

bleeding in the parking lot

        of the high school   during sixth period

earth science class

                      as we crowd the window,

her blonde hair   flickering

like wind-caught snow,

the teacher vanishing   down the hall,

snow dissolving Jane's

                                        body on the pavement.

How, as girls, no one

        told us what was happening,   not with words, but we felt

the sirens
                as a kind of voice.   How we even survive

the danger of roses.   Then a stone in the lake, an arbitrary number, the news on the television   where my turning

takes place, a wall of round names   and lips, one clock

after another

                babbling the litany. How I have

no place,   but this small oracle, ash

from the synagogues,   a gust of wind

                ruffling the sheaves of paper.

Twentieth-Century Novel

When the war is over the cows lower in the field like sad mothers.

Then the goats emerge from a twentieth-century novel.

The beginning of a famous grief-song.

The lark's notes walk you down the sea-shell avenue.

Ancestors steaming in a red-hot bowl.

That's what the goats are for, sings the lark.

The cow's firetongue hangs in air sticky with poison.

The cows are at work planning their first garden.

The tulip's cardiac flame.

The goats chew the ivy curving through the spine, inventing you.

At the CarMax in Maryland to Sell Your Used Civic That Doesn't Have Air Conditioning but was Your Grandmother's and the Only Place You've Ever Owned

You are distracted.

You love rain when there is none.

You hate November with its dying sun.

You look out the window because it makes you sad.

You love this car though it's gone bad.

Bad like an apple.

Bad like your blues.

You hold the pen like an apple

distracted by blues.

You hate rain when there is none.

You love November with its dying sun.

You look out the window to the empty lot.

    Sign here, says the salesman.

    I'm giving you all I've got.

Eden in Foreclosure

Farm Fresh Apples swings the wooden sign above
a crowded barrel where Eurydice stands, shoulders

leaned back against the bright wind blowing
in between people, but she is distracted, staring sadly

at her chipped nail-polished thumb, something emboldening
then dimming like smoke in the mind.

One must have her mind of winter
in a world without form, the great fires

lurking the treetops, sun diminishing
behind the leaves like an ancient whale

within a lurid, holographic second mid-air.
She thinks to touch the apple, but can't, not

like the way it once was, description
falling from her mouth like bad teeth.

The man behind the fruit stand waves weightlessly,
his tree-lined rib floating freely without string.

It hurts to remember the apple
born blondly from the earth into speech.

New World: Eurydice

I wanted to return to the garden, but it is too late,
the confusing stars, the evening too cold
to travel through. I prefer
where I am, the controlling present,
braiding and unbraiding my hair in the dark,
no longer a reaction, but closer
to the question, a vehicle for thought driving
a strange bristling in the underbrush.

If it meant someone else would have a better life
I wouldn't mind dying, says the voice
in this dream, the azalea blistering
like a lit match, bulbs of dahlias
gesturing from underground.

You are with me in the garden, it is saying now,
the voice is speaking, though only the wind
motions toward me.

If I had a soul, the soul is what I am now.
If I say its name, I, a glittering
extension of God, possess it.

A Legend and Its Context

If the saint grows famous,

                if the prayer house

prospers, the service becoming more

                        elaborate, more detailed,
                        a shadowed wing

swinging behind stained glass

             like a scythe. If she

                        is tired and desires to break
                        his bones in bed, if his bones

are hers, a sudden shift in the singular

                        possessive, to be her-

self, suddenly, on the street, carrying

                              the groceries, the rotting fruit,

a sermon of pollen

masking the wind.

                  A woman is an archive of weather

                  or the tongue cut out.

If the saint is wind and the glass tree grows

through the roof

              and the root is the tongue, her mouth.

Borges Sells Me the Apple, Sells Me the World

The dream came back, and I split in two.

My father flickers gold in the driveway.

He is a tree beginning in the yard of the house.

The garden ends in the window of his arms.

Someone weeps for Noah, hollers his name.

(You can tell by the oblivious eyes, head turned briefly, the mouth's gesture.)

I name all my dreams The Father.

He understands he is an illusion, someone else is dreaming him.

In the driveway, Adam kisses the snake and becomes a rose.

Eve yawns, counting the beetles.

The dream was so close to the surface, it banged its head on the floorboards.

I trespass forever in the unflinching past.

The apple's a for-sale sign swaying from the tree.

Notes

The poem "After Translating the Women of the 20th Century" pays homage to the buried history of Eastern European, Jewish, German-language, women poets of the 20th century, and is also a tribute, particularly, to Selma Meerbaum-Eisinger and Rose Ausländer. Through translating their poems I see, through language, a world that lives inside our language. The image "lipsticked girl" is from Seamus Heaney's poem "Song." The line "This winter I want a house (In diesen Winter brauch ich ein Haus)" is from Sarah Kirsch's poem "Weites Haus / Large House" from the anthology *German Poetry 1910-1975*, selected, translated, and introduced by Michael Hamburger.

The lines "You must imagine Eurydice / happy" from the poem "A Condo for Sale Overlooking the Cemetery in Kearny, NJ" are inspired by Albert Camus' essay "The Myth of Sisyphus" and its conclusion: "Each atom of that stone, each mineral flake of that night filled a mountain, in itself forms a world. The struggle itself toward the heights is enough to fill a man's heart. One must imagine Sisyphus happy."

Both poems entitled "Borges Sells Me the Apple, Sells Me the World" draw inspiration from Jorge Luis Borges' collected Charles Eliot Norton lectures, 1967-1968, *This Craft of Verse*, edited by Călin-Andrei Mihăilesu.

"Memory of France" is inspired by Paul Celan's poem of the same title translated from the German by Monika Zobel and published in *In the Shape of a Human Body I Am Visiting the Earth*, edited by Ilya Kaminsky, Dominic Luxford, and Jesse Nathan. The second poem titled "Borges Sells Me the Apple, Sells Me the World" draws from lines in "Under the Floorboards" by Rachel Hadas: "The dream was so close to the surface / it almost bumped its head on the dusty floorboards," a poem also found in this anthology.

"The Wolves Ran on Through the Evergreen Forests" is a line from W.H. Auden's "In Memory of W.B Yeats."

"I'll Give This Letter to a Worm" is speech from Sarah Ruhl's *Eurydice* libretto. In movement 3, scene 3, right at the end of the opera, Eurydice writes a letter to Orpheus and "her husband's next wife" and before signing off she says: "I'll give this letter to a worm. I hope he finds you." She then places the letter on the ground and dips herself into the River Lethe.

In "The Townspeople Contemplate Eurydice," "the Russian poet" is a reference to Russian Romantic poet Mikhail Lermontov's untitled poem, translated by Yevgeny Bonver, in which the speaker expresses the desire to be buried alive "And the oak, evergreen and shady, / Would decline to me and rustle above." In the poem "Reading Virginia Woolf in a Women in Literature Class at Bergen Community College," the lines "fishing-boats against the moon" and "giant artichokes towered among roses" are from Woolf's *To the Lighthouse*. The final lines are borrowed and slightly altered from a letter she wrote to Violet Dickinson on August 3, 1912: "We shall be back in October. At first we shall stay at Brunswick Sq: but we hope to take rooms somewhere this week. Everything has been left to the last—but the Novels are finished—and that is a great relief. In October we shall read them over, and decide whether they are to go straight into Hell." The "we" here references Leonard Woolf, whom she married on August 10, 1912.

In "Moses in Brooklyn," the lines "what is unwritten, hardened / into language, lays bare a sky" are from Paul Celan's poem "A La Pointe Acérée" from *No One's Rose*, translated from the German by David Young. The French title, as noted by Young, "translates as 'with a steel-sharp point' or 'in a pointed manner.'"

In "Driving Through Maspeth, NY, After Teaching an Introduction to Creative Writing Class," the Anne Sexton reference is to her poem "Cigarettes And Whiskey And Wild, Wild Women."

In "Teaching the Persona Poem at Ramapo College of New Jersey," the Ai reference is to her poem "The Kid." The Martin Buber reference is to his book *I and Thou*.

In "A Year Made Out of a Cut in Your Civilization," the line "blond-haired spring" references an image in my translation from the German of Rose Ausländer's poem "On the Steps of Heaven."

The second poem titled "The Twenty-First Century" draws inspiration from Charles Wright's poem "Broken English": "Truth's an indefinite article. / When we live, we live for the last time, / as Akhmatova says, / One *the* in a world of *a*."

"Refurbished Eden" is inspired by Aharon Appelfeld's memoir *The Story of a Life*.

In "Mary Magdalene, Mary Oliver, & Me," the lines "true as Mary Magdalene / creature of desire" are lyrics from FKA Twig's "Mary Magdalene." The final couplet borrows and relineates lines from Mary Oliver's poem "Knife."

"Rose Ausländer, Jane Roe, & Me," borrows from my translations from the German of various poems by Rose Ausländer (1901–1988), a Jewish, German-language poet and translator, born in what was then Austria and is now known as Czernowitz in Ukraine. She is the recipient of several German literary awards, including the Droste Prize of Meersburg (1967), the Ida-Dehmel Prize, the Andreas-Gryphius Prize, the Roswitha-Medallion of Bad Gandersheim (1980), and the Literature Prize of the Bavarian Academy of Art (1984). Ausländer, who mostly lived between Eastern Europe, New York City, and Düsseldorf, is the author of over a dozen books of poetry. She died in the Nelly Sacks House in Düsseldorf on January 3, 1988. This poem is a response to the June 2022 Supreme Court overturning of *Roe v. Wade*.

The line "One must have her mind of winter" in "Eden in Foreclosure" derives from Wallace Stevens' poem "The Snow Man." The image "born blondly" is an homage to Lucie Brock-Broido's line "kissed him blondly / On his mouth" from her poem "Currying the Fallow-Colored Horse."

Acknowledgments

Thank you to the editors of the following publications who have published poems from this collection, sometimes in different forms:

The Academy of American Poets, Brazenhead Review, Breaking the Glass: A Contemporary Jewish Poetry Anthology (Laurel Review), Brink Literary, The Common, The Massachusetts Review, New England Review, Peste Magazine, Pigeon Pages, and *Poetry Northwest.*

Thank you to Martha Rhodes, Ryan Murphy, Jonathan Blunk, and Four Way Books for being a dream team and home.

Thank you, particularly, to Hannah Matheson, for your editorial brilliance and careful attention to these poems. I am profoundly grateful.

For your light, love, and faith in all worlds: Johnny Steers.

Thank you for your friendship and generosity, for lending an ear and eye: Binnie Kirshenbaum, Anna Rose Welch, Elizabeth Metzger, Michelle Delaney, Meghan Maguire Dahn. Ariel Francisco Henriquez Cos: no poems without you.

For my mother, Barbara Cecille Barmann Hoffman—my twentieth- and twenty-first-century woman.

About the Author

Carlie Hoffman is the author of the poetry collections *One More World Like This World* (Four Way Books, 2025); *When There Was Light* (Four Way Books, 2023), winner of the National Jewish Book Award; and *This Alaska* (Four Way Books, 2021), winner of the Northern California Publishers & Authors Gold Award in Poetry as well as a finalist for the Foreword INDIES Book of the Year Award. Hoffman is the translator from the German of both Selma Meerbaum-Eisinger's *Blütenlese* (World Poetry Books, 2026) and *White Shadows: Anneliese Hager and the Camera-less Photograph* (Atelier Éditions, 2025), as well as the poems of Rose Ausländer. Hoffman's other honors include a 92NY "Discovery" / *Boston Review* prize and a *Poets & Writers* Amy Award. She is the founder and editor-in-chief of *Small Orange Journal*.

WE ARE ALSO GRATEFUL TO THOSE INDIVIDUALS WHO PARTICIPATED IN OUR
BUILD A BOOK PROGRAM. THEY ARE:

Anonymous (14), Robert Abrams, Debra Allbery, Nancy Allen,
Michael Ansara, Kathy Aponick, Jean Ball, Sally Ball, Jill Bialosky,
Sophie Cabot Black, Laurel Blossom, Tommye Blount, Karen and
David Blumenthal, Jonathan Blunk, Lee Briccetti, Jane Martha Brox,
Mary Lou Buschi, Anthony Cappo, Carla and Steven Carlson,
Robin Rosen Chang, Liza Charlesworth, Peter Coyote,
Elinor Cramer, Kwame Dawes, Michael Anna de Armas,
Brian Komei Dempster, Renko and Stuart Dempster,
Matthew DeNichilo, Rosalynde Vas Dias, Patrick Donnelly,
Charles R. Douthat, Lynn Emanuel, Blas Falconer, Laura Fjeld,
Carolyn Forché, Helen Fremont and Donna Thagard,
Debra Gitterman, Dorothy Tapper Goldman, Alison Granucci,
Elizabeth T. Gray Jr., Naomi Guttman and Jonathan Mead,
Jeffrey Harrison, KT Herr, Carlie Hoffman, Melissa Hotchkiss,
Thomas and Autumn Howard, Catherine Hoyser, Elizabeth Jackson,
Linda Susan Jackson, Jessica Jacobs, Deborah Jonas-Walsh,
Jennifer Just, Voki Kalfayan, Maeve Kinkead, Victoria Korth,
David Lee and Jamila Trindle, Rodney Terich Leonard,
Howard Levy, Owen Lewis and Susan Ennis, Eve Linn,
Matthew Lippman, Ralph and Mary Ann Lowen, Maja Lukic,
Neal Lulofs, Anthony Lyons, Ricardo Alberto Maldonado,
Trish Marshall, Donna Masini, Deborah McAlister, Carol Moldaw,
Michael and Nancy Murphy, Kimberly Nunes, Matthew Olzmann and
Vievee Francis, Veronica Patterson, Patrick Phillips, Robert Pinsky,
Megan Pinto, Kevin Prufer, Anna Duke Reach, Paula Rhodes,
Yoana Setzer, James Shalek, Soraya Shalforoosh, Peggy Shinner,
Joan Silber, Jane Simon, Debra Spark, Donna Spruijt-Metz,
Arlene Stang, Page Hill Starzinger, Catherine Stearns,
Yerra Sugarman, Arthur Sze, Laurence Tancredi, Marjorie and
Lew Tesser, Peter Turchi, Connie Voisine, Susan Walton,
Martha Webster and Robert Fuentes, Calvin Wei, Allison Benis White,
Lauren Yaffe, and Rolf Yngve.